THE OLD

Point Loma Lighthouse

CABRILLO NATIONAL MONUMENT

Cabrillo National Monument Foundation

1800 Cabrillo Memorial Drive
San Diego, California 92106

Library of Congress Cataloging-in-Publication Data
Holland, F. Ross (Francis Ross), 1927–2005.
    The Old Point Loma Lighthouse / F. Ross Holland. —3rd ed.
      p. cm.
    ISBN 978-0-941032-09-4 (pbk. : alk. paper)
      1. Lighthouses—California—Loma, Point—History. I. Title.

    VK1025.P6H6 2006
    387.1'550974985—dc22

                                        2006047077

Third Edition 2007
Written by F. Ross Holland
Designed and produced by Amanda Summers, Prescott, AZ
Edited by Paula Degen
CNMF Project Coordinator: Karen Eccles
Printed in the U.S.A.

CREDITS:
The Bancroft Library, University of California, Berkeley: 5, 23, 24; Richard Cummins 4; Kim Fahlen 16, 18;
Cabrillo National Monument, NPS: 7, 8 (map), 14 (bottom), 15, 17 (bottom), 25, 27, 28, 29, 34, 35,
36, 37 (diagram), 39 (top), 41, 42 (top), 44, 45, 46 (top); Library of Congress: 8, 10, 43; National Archives: 11,
13, 14 (top); PictureHistory.com 22; San Diego Historical Society: 1, 3 (lighthouse), 21, 32, 37, 39 (bottom), 40,
42 (middle, bottom); San Diego Maritime Museum: 9; Scripps Institution of Oceanography Archives: 30 (top);
Dan Spinella Artworks 18 (top); Thomas A. Tag, U.S.Lighthouse Society: 17 (top); Henry Wakefield: cover, 12;
Nancy Parkinson Munson: 30 (bottom), 31, 33, 36 (shell frame and detail); Gordon Wolford: 47.

ABOUT CABRILLO NATIONAL MONUMENT FOUNDATION

Cabrillo National Monument Foundation is a nonprofit organization dedicated, in cooperation with the
National Park Service, to supporting the preservation and enhancement of the natural, cultural, historical,
scientific, and educational resources of Cabrillo National Monument. Chartered in 1956, the Foundation is
governed by a volunteer board of directors.

If you are interested in becoming a member, please contact us at:
    Cabrillo National Monument Foundation
    1800 Cabrillo Memorial Drive
    San Diego, California, 92106
    619-222-4747
    www.cnmf.org

This book is printed on Endeavour Velvet paper, 50% recycled, 25% post-consumer waste, and certified by the Forest Stewardship
Council. We've chosen to use this paper to reinforce our belief in the importance of environmental responsibility and to inspire
others to help conserve the earth's precious resources. Even small conservation efforts go a long way towards the larger goal of
environmental preservation.

CABRILLO NATIONAL MONUMENT owes its popularity to several distinctly different attractions: It overlooks the site of the landing in 1542 of Juan Rodríguez Cabrillo on what is now the west coast of the United States; it has a public observatory for watching the annual migration of gray whales; its unusual tidepools offer a fascinating view of life forms from the ocean below; its Mediterranean climate supports remarkably diverse habitats, offering opportunities for birding, wildlife watching, and enjoying springtime wildflowers; it provides a panoramic view of city, mountain, bay, and sea that rates among the finest in the world; and it has the Old Point Loma Lighthouse, one of the earliest U.S. Government lighthouses on the Pacific Coast.

CONTENTS

This book about the Old Point Loma Lighthouse was written by F. Ross Holland, who was the first park historian at Cabrillo National Monument, 1959 to 1964. Holland worked at numerous national parks and in research and planning positions during a 33-year career with the National Park Service. He received the Department of the Interior Meritorious Service Award for his contributions to historic

preservation. From the American Lighthouse Coordinating Committee he received the Distinguished Service Award for contributions to the history and preservation of the nation's lighthouses.

Holland retired from the National Park Service in 1983 to pursue interests in writing and consulting. The author of numerous books on lighthouses—among them: *America's Lighthouses: An Illustrated History* (1972), *Great American Lighthouses* (1994), *Lighthouses* (1995), and *Maryland Lighthouses of the Chesapeake Bay* (1997)—Holland has been called the "dean" of American lighthouse historians. He died in 2005 at the age of 78.

His book on San Diego's Old Point Loma Lighthouse was published originally in 1968 and revised in 1978. Revised again in 2007, this latest version updates the story of the famous lighthouse to reflect what today's visitors to Cabrillo National Monument can see and experience.

INTRODUCTION

In 1854 a contractor's crew from the eastern United States came to San Diego to build the port's first lighthouse. They worked hard and built well. The brick and sandstone structure they erected survived the onslaught of storms, earthquakes, neglect, and vandalism, and today still stands, with most of its original material intact.

For 36 years this Cape Cod-style lighthouse, near the end of a long, high peninsula called Point Loma, guided ships along the coast of California and into San Diego Harbor. But the real story is not that of a lighthouse faithfully performing its task—all lighthouses do that. The real significance of the old structure is in its creation.

The lighthouse at Point Loma was one of the first eight lighthouses along the Pacific Coast of the United States. All eight were built by one firm under one contract. The Old Point Loma Lighthouse stands today as a symbol of the nation's first successful effort to obtain navigational aids for the newly acquired west coast.

Fundamental changes in the nation's aids to navigation and their administration were taking place in the 1850s. Many of the problems of modernization of the lighthouse system were reflected in the establishment and early years of the Pacific Coast's first lighthouses.

Prior to the American Revolution the individual colonies erected, maintained, and operated lighthouses within their territories. But shortly after the establishment of the United States, Congress passed an act on August 7, 1789, assuming central responsibility for lighthouses and other aids to navigation. Between 1789 and 1795 the states turned over their lighthouses to the Federal Government.

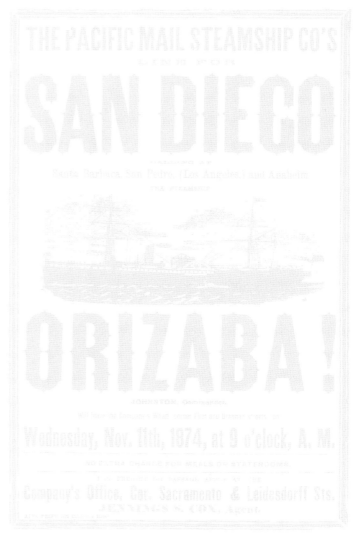

Ships have long been an efficient way to move goods and passengers along the West Coast. With its naval activity, marine commerce, and cruise lines, San Diego is one of the nation's busiest ports.

The duty of supervising lighthouses and other navigational aids was vested in the Secretary of the U.S. Treasury and the Commissioner of Revenue until 1820 when the task of supervising all aids to navigation was assigned to the Fifth Auditor of the U.S. Treasury Department. This arrangement proved unsatisfactory and, in 1851, Congress appointed a board to study the lighthouse problem. Its lengthy report recommended appointing a permanent lighthouse board to administer navigational aids throughout the United States.

Congress acted on this recommendation in 1852 and established a nine-member board, with the Secretary of the Treasury as president. The Lighthouse Board divided the country into twelve districts; the Pacific Coast was the 12th Lighthouse District. An inspector appointed in each district was charged with "building the lighthouses, with keeping them in repair, and with the purchase, the setting up, and the repairs of the illuminating apparatus."

Direct supervision of lighthouses devolved upon the various collectors of customs. Collectors who had lighthouses in their district also held the appointive job of superintendent of lighthouses. By 1854, O. S. Witherby, the collector of customs for San Diego, was appointed superintendent of lights for Point Loma and Point Conception to the north.

The story of the Old Point Loma Lighthouse begins at the time of significant changes in the nation's lighthouse administration and also the time of increasing demands for lighting the newly acquired California coast. It is a story that goes beyond the rise and demise of this landmark to illuminate the vital place of lighthouses in our maritime heritage. The Old Point Loma Lighthouse is also important as a reminder of simpler times. It is a window to the past and the lives of men and women at outposts along the nation's shorelines who faithfully tended the lights that guided mariners.

"I can think of no other edifice constructed by man as altruistic as a lighthouse. They were built only to serve. They weren't built for any other purpose."

— GEORGE BERNARD SHAW

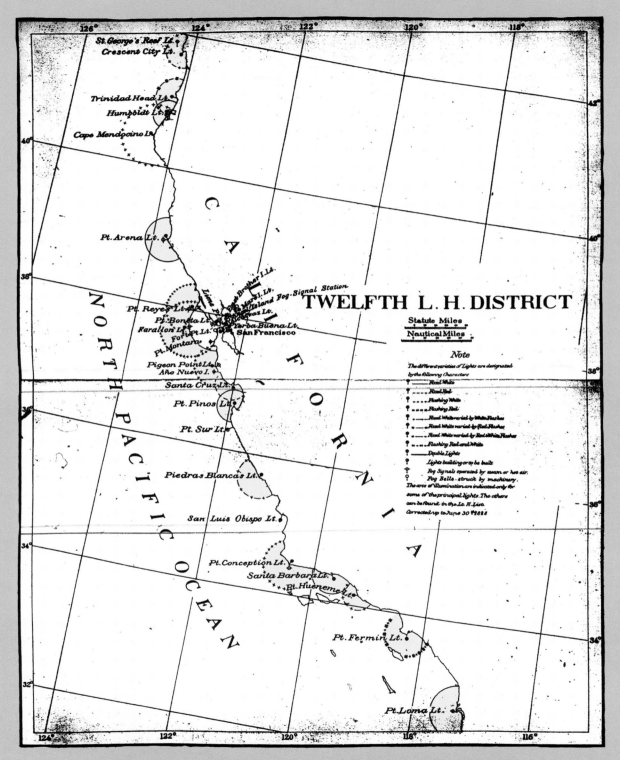

1888 MAP OF THE 12TH LIGHTHOUSE DISTRICT

THE SETTING

Point Loma is a long finger of land protecting San Diego Harbor on the west. Its high crest ranges from about 300 feet above sea level to 422 feet where the old lighthouse stands. On its western side, where the Pacific Ocean crashes furiously against its edge forming a rugged coastline, Point Loma slopes gently back several thousand feet and then rises sharply to the undulating crest. On the bay side it falls off precipitously to about 100 feet above sea level where once again it gently slopes to the water's edge. The view from Point Loma is one of the great harbor views in the world, taking in a vast panorama of sea, islands, coast, San Diego skyline, harbor, and mountains.

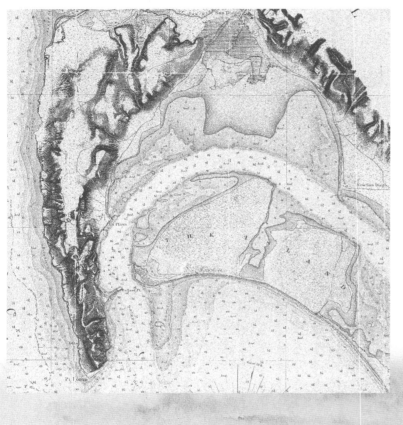

When construction of the lighthouse began in 1854, Point Loma was virtually uninhabited. There was some fishing and whaling activity at Ballast Point and La Playa, about five miles away. There were no roads. Only trails—probably originally used by the native Kumeyaay Indians—sliced through the chaparral.

The view was as spectacular then as it is today. To the north and east, small clusters of houses and other buildings could be seen here and there. San Diego essentially consisted of Old Town, then only a village. The 1850 Census recorded the urban population of San Diego as 650—a multi-ethnic mix of European, Spanish, Mexican, African, Asian, Hawaiian, Filipino, and native. Part of North Island was under water, especially at high tide. The shores of the harbor were less regular than today, and rowboats tied up where Pacific Highway now runs.

There was little need for navigational aids in the early part of the 19th century because few ships traveled the coast. For a few years soldiers at Fort Guijarros, a Spanish cannon battery, maintained a small light beacon on the tip of Ballast Point, but by 1810 this early Point Loma light had washed away. There are reports that during Mexican rule in the 1820s and 1830s, a lantern was hung on a stake at Ballast Point when a supply ship was expected from Mexico. Ship traffic to the California coast increased as the Gold Rush in 1849 and the 1850s brought prospectors, settlers, and merchants seeking new opportunities. With the increase in shipping came increasing calls for permanent aids for navigation.

In 1851, a year after California entered the Union, the U.S. Coast Survey selected the heights of Point Loma for the site of a navigational aid. The location seemed ideal. Here its light would command the surrounding area, piercing the darkness far out to sea, warning of the rocky coast below, and leading mariners safely into the protected natural harbor of San Diego Bay.

SELECTING SITES FOR THE WEST COAST LIGHTS

Mexico ceded California to the United States in 1848, and almost immediately western shippers urged Congress to provide navigational aids along the Pacific Coast. Congress authorized several lighthouses in the bill that established the Oregon Territory in 1848, but more were needed. Two years later, on September 28, 1850, the 308th anniversary of Juan Rodríguez Cabrillo's arrival at San Diego Bay, Congress authorized additional lighthouses. Three lighthouses were approved for the Washington coast: Cape Flattery, Cape Disappointment, and New Dungeness. Six were authorized for California: Alcatraz Island and Battery (or Fort) Point in San Francisco Bay; Farallon Islands off San Francisco; Point Pinos near Monterey; Point Conception; and San Diego.

*I*n 1843, Alexander Dallas Bache (1806–1867), great-grandson of Benjamin Franklin and a leading scientist and educator, was appointed by President Tyler to head the United States Coast Survey. Bache supervised mapping and data collection for all the coasts and introduced such new technologies as the electric telegraph and photography into the process.

The U.S. Coast Survey was responsible for selecting the actual sites for the new lighthouses. On May 29, 1851, the first issue of San Diego's first newspaper, the *Herald,* carried this announcement:

> *The officers of the U.S. Coast Survey are now actively engaged in the survey of the Harbor preparatory to the selection of a site for the Government Light House at this point.*

The next month, A. M. Harrison, chief topographer of the party, wrote to the superintendent of the Coast Survey, Alexander D. Bache, to recommend a spot near the end of Point Loma, 422 feet above sea level, as the site for the lighthouse. He said materials could be landed at La Playa and easily hauled to the site. It would be necessary to bring in all materials for the structure because, he noted, there was "nothing in the region which could be turned to advantage."

In what seemed an afterthought, Harrison mentioned that during his stay the fogs were frequent and heavy. Bache wrote back to ask whether the high point recommended by Harrison would result in the fog too frequently interfering in the normal functioning of the light. Harrison replied that fog might be somewhat of a problem, but the Point Loma site was still the best choice. Bache concurred and transmitted the site recommendation to the Secretary of the Treasury.

Major Hartman Bache, uncle of Alexander D. Bache, believed there should be a drawing of each lighthouse for the archives of the Lighthouse Board. He sketched each structure as he inspected it. A draftsman in San Francisco then rendered the sketches into finished drawings. Many of these drawings from 1855–1859 have since disappeared, but photographs of them have survived and are now in the National Archives.

TOP TO BOTTOM:
Point Pinos Lighthouse
Point Conception Lighthouse
Farallon Islands Lighthouse
Alcatraz Island Lighthouse

The site selected for the Point Loma light seemed ideal. The combined height of the bluff and the tower made it the highest lighthouse in the country. But its height was its undoing, because fog and low-lying clouds frequently obscured the beacon.

Bache's hunch proved correct. Forty years later, in 1891, the Point Loma light was moved to a much lower position, solely because fog frequently obscured the higher light. At the time, however, Harrison chose the only site that would permit the lighthouse to serve as a coastal light and to some extent as a harbor light, both of which were needed for San Diego.

The Federal Government was interested in the Point Loma site for another reason. In 1852 the Secretary of War recommended to President Millard Fillmore that a military reservation be set aside there

> *to include that portion of the Peninsula lying on the west side of the entrance to the Harbor, which shall be included between the southernmost point of the peninsula (Punta de Soma [Loma]) and a line drawn across said peninsula from the harbor to the Ocean at the distance of one and a half miles above Punta de Guanos [Guijarros].*

President Fillmore approved and ordered the establishment of the military reservation which would become Fort Rosecrans. The reservation included the site that the Coast Survey had selected for the Point Loma lighthouse; however, the site was not officially reserved for lighthouse purposes until September 11, 1854.

12

BUILDING THE LIGHTHOUSES

After some difficulty the Secretary of the Treasury located a Baltimore, Maryland, firm interested in building lighthouses along the Pacific Coast. The firm's two partners, Francis A. Gibbons and Francis X. Kelly, entered into an agreement with the Federal Government on April 20, 1852, to construct lighthouses at eight locations: Alcatraz Island, Battery Point (Fort Point), Southeast Farallon Island, Humboldt Harbor, Monterey, Point Conception, and San Diego on the California coast and at Cape Disappointment at the mouth of the Columbia River. They were to receive $15,000 for each of the California lighthouses, payable as each lighthouse was completed and accepted. For the Cape Disappointment lighthouse, they were to receive $31,000—a total of $136,000 for all eight lighthouses. Completion was due by November 1, 1853, but a supplement to the contract later extended the time to May 1, 1854.

The contractors purchased in Baltimore a bark named *Oriole*, 1,223 tons burden, to transport materials and workers to the West Coast. They hired 14 tradesmen in Baltimore: 2 bricklayers, 2 carpenters, 1 painter, 1 blacksmith, 1 plasterer and bricklayer, 2 stonemasons, and 5 workmen. In addition, they employed William H. Hemmick as clerk and disbursing agent; Roger J. Mahon "to superintend the building of [the] eight lighthouses;" and William J. Timanus to act as contractors' agent, keeping the books and making "all disbursements and purchases connected with the work. . . ."

Cape Disappointment was an apt name for the lighthouse at the mouth of the Columbia River, shown in this 1859 Bache drawing. The ship carrying construction materials sank here in 1853, delaying completion of the final four lighthouses.

All the materials and hired tradesmen for building the lighthouses, except the brick and lime, were collected and loaded aboard *Oriole*. The ship departed Baltimore August 12, 1852, and arrived in San Francisco January 29, 1853. An advance party had arrived a month earlier to lay foundations for the Alcatraz and Fort Point lighthouses. Work began in earnest with the arrival of the main party, and within a few months both lighthouses in San Francisco Bay were completed, followed by the lighthouses on Farallon Island and then Point Pinos.

The contractors next headed for Cape Disappointment, aptly named, it seems. Misfortune struck when *Oriole* hit a rock and sank in the mouth of the Columbia River, taking with her all the material for the remaining four lighthouses. Fortunately, no lives were lost. The disaster delayed them, of course, but as rapidly as they could, the contractors gathered more material and went about completing their contract.

The first drawing of the Old Point Loma Lighthouse, made by Major Hartman Bache shortly after it was built in 1855, shows the road from Ballast Point.

Gibbons and Kelly did not relish the idea of building the lighthouse on top of Point Loma. To reach the site they had to hack a road up the side of the hill through tangled chaparral, haul supplies up from Ballast Point, and haul in water from La Playa.

The neighboring communities at Ballast Point and La Playa are notable for their ethnic diversity at a time when much of California was racially segregated. The ancient maritime traditions that enabled Portuguese, English, Chinese, African, and other ethnic groups to live in close quarters on ships were apparent in the whaling and fishing trades on the Point Loma peninsula.

La Playa

Ballast Point

Point Loma Lighthouse

To expedite work, they placed the Cape Disappointment and Humboldt Harbor construction under the supervision of Mahon, and designated Timanus to supervise work at Point Conception and San Diego.

The location of the Point Loma lighthouse was a matter of dispute. The Coast Survey party had selected a site near the end of Point Loma, but the contract with Gibbons and Kelly merely specified "San Diego." The contractors objected to the Point Loma location because of the cost of building a road and bridges to haul materials to the site.

After considerable arguing with the Lighthouse Board, and rejecting an option to drop their contract, Gibbons and Kelly finally proceeded with construction on Point Loma in April 1854.

Meanwhile as the lights farther north were completed, people in San Diego began wondering when their turn would come. In 1853 the editor of the local paper complained: "The appropriation was made by Congress some three years ago, and as yet, there has not been a blow struck." Nearly another year passed before that first blow was finally struck for the Point Loma light.

On April 7, 1854, the schooner *Vaquero* arrived from San Francisco with materials for Point Loma, and work began a few days later. Bricks, cement, lime, and lumber were hauled from *Vaquero* at Ballast Point to the top of Point Loma over a road that had taken 18 of the contractors' men 35 days to construct. The bricks were used for the tower. Sandstone for the dwelling was obtained on Point Loma, apparently from a quarry near Ballast Point. Tiles for the basement floor came from the ruins of the old Spanish Fort Guijarros at Ballast Point. There was no water on the chaparral-covered summit of Point Loma to moisten the mortar and plaster, so the builders had to haul water from a well at La Playa, a distance of about seven miles.

A reporter for the San Diego *Herald* visited the site during the construction. Timanus gave him this description of what the structure would be when completed:

The walls will be 20 feet high from the foundation, and the entire building 20 feet wide by 30 feet long. There will be a cellar of 6 feet in the

Original drawings of the lighthouse show the center tower that is characteristic of the Cape Cod style. The dwelling was simple and functional. The 22-inch-thick sandstone walls kept it cool in summer and held in the warmth of the fireplace and kitchen stove in the winter. Water for cooking and washing was pumped up from the basement cistern.

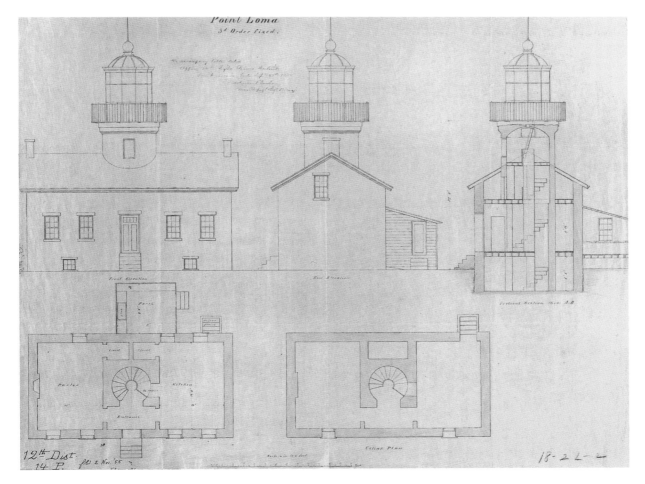

clear, the main building will be 9 feet 2 inches in the clear, and the attic 3 1/2 feet. The "tower" will be situated directly in the middle of the building and will be 10 feet in diameter, thus leaving on each side rooms of 14 to 20 feet. A spiral stair case will lead through the tower to its height, which is to be 33 feet from its base, thus there will be an elevation of 433 (actually 462) feet from the level of the sea. A kitchen and other out offices are also to be erected of wood in the rear, and when completed will form a useful ornament.

The tower protruding from the center of the keeper's dwelling was a characteristic of the Cape Cod design—named for its eastern counterpart—and was typical of the style of the early California lighthouses.

No accounts of the actual construction exist. It was completed sometime prior to August 26, 1854—the date when the collector of customs in San Diego reported to the Lighthouse Board that the inspector had examined and received the lighthouse on behalf of the Federal Government. The final cost was nearly double the initial estimate of $15,000, due, no doubt, to the difficulty of hauling materials to the site.

Outfitted with a Fresnel lens—the best available technology—the Old Point Loma Lighthouse served as both a harbor light and a coastal light during its 36 years of active service.

THE LIGHTING CONTROVERSY

Until the 1850s, nearly every lighthouse in the United States used Argand lamps and parabolic reflectors for illumination. The lamps were placed side by side around the circumference of a circle. The number of lamps used depended upon the arc of the horizon it was to illuminate. For many years a bull's-eye magnifying lens was used on each lamp, but these lenses proved ineffective, and in 1840 they were removed, leaving the reflectors.

This American system, as it was known, had only one apparent virtue: the lamps were inexpensive. On the other

hand, they had several weaknesses: they were complicated; they used a vast amount of oil; they required constant attention; and, most important, they produced relatively little light.

In 1822 Augustin Fresnel (1788–1827), a French physicist, developed a lens apparatus that would revolutionize lighthouse illumination. A Fresnel lens is like a glass barrel whose outer surface is made up of prisms and bull's-eyes. In a revolving or flashing light, the bull's-eyes are surrounded by curved, concentric prisms, concentrating the light of a central lamp into several individual beams, radiating like the spokes of a wheel. In the fixed, or steady light, the bull's-eyes become a continuous "lens belt," with the prisms parallel to it, producing an uninterrupted, horizontal sheet of light.

One of a series of Argand lamp burners that illuminated early American lighthouses.

Fresnel lenses were classified into seven orders, or sizes. The order was determined by focal distance—the distance from the light source to the inside surface of the lens. The first order was the largest and had the greatest range; the sixth order was the smallest.

ORDER	FOCAL DISTANCE MILLIMETERS	INCHES	OVERALL LENS SIZE DIAMETER IN FEET
First	920	36.2	6.0
Second	700	27.6	4.5
Third	500	19.7	3.17
Three and a Half	375	14.7	2.4
Fourth	250	9.8	1.5
Fifth	187.5	7.4	1.17
Sixth	150	5.9	.83

Augustin Fresnel was famous for the lighting system that carries his name.

The United States was slow to adopt the Fresnel lenses. For years there was controversy in this country over the merits of the old and new systems. In 1841, the United States installed its first Fresnel lens at Navesink Light, New Jersey, as a test. The Fifth Auditor of the Treasury dragged out the experiments on Argand versus Fresnel for 10 years. However, support for the Fresnel system was growing. An appropriation bill passed by Congress on March 3, 1851, included permission for the Secretary of the Treasury to place the Fresnel lens system in new lighthouses, in lighthouses that did not yet have lenses, and in lighthouses requiring new lenses.

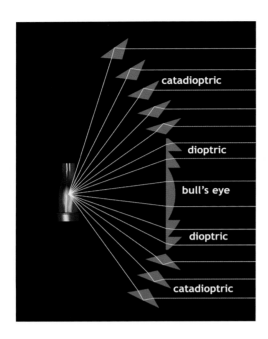

The Fresnel lens is an ingenious system of glass prisms and bull's-eye lenses that collect and direct light rays to form a single powerful beam. As suggested in the illustration above, the catadioptric prisms refract and reflect; the dioptric prisms and center bull's-eye refract. A first order lens had more than 1,000 prisms and could send its beam dozens of miles if set high enough. For maximum effect, the light had to compensate for the curvature of the earth. A light high above sea level could be seen farther than if it were at the water's edge.

A year later the board that had been created to study the lighthouse system concluded: "The Fresnel lens is greatly superior to any other mode of lighthouse illumination, and in point of economy is nearly four times as advantageous as the best system of reflectors and Argand lamps." In May 1852 the first chairman of the Lighthouse Board said: "[The] Fresnel Lens in useful effect, brilliancy and economy is superior in its different orders to any combination, number and size of the best parabolic reflectors."

Despite this strong support for the Fresnel lens, the Fifth Auditor of the Treasury clung tenaciously to his Argand lamps. As late as 1852, in what was one of his last acts as general superintendent of lights, he recommended that the proposed lighthouse at San Diego be illuminated with the old system, using 12 lamps and 12, 16-inch reflectors.

With the establishment of the Lighthouse Board in 1852, however, proponents of the Fresnel apparatus were in a position to carry out the intent of Congress and install the new system. By 1859 the changeover from the Argand lamp and reflector system to the Fresnel lenses throughout the United States was almost complete.

The lower consumption of oil and other virtues of the Fresnel lenses made up for the higher initial cost of the system. In addition, the Fresnel equipment was nearly foolproof. A lighthouse keeper could hardly make a mistake. As one historian noted:

The adoption in this country of the Fresnel Lenticular apparatus made it possible for a light keeper of average capacity to keep a good light, and impossible for him to keep a bad one, unless by violation of plain rules and avoidance of routine duties.

The Secretary of the Treasury dispatched Lt. Washington A. Bartlett, USN, to France to contract for the manufacture of Fresnel illuminating apparatuses for the Pacific Coast lighthouses. Shortly after arriving in Paris, Bartlett entered into a contract with Sautter & Co. to manufacture two, third order illuminating apparatuses: one for the Fort Point lighthouse and one for the Alcatraz Island lighthouse at San Francisco.

Bartlett then got permission to contract with Sautter & Co. for the other six illuminating apparatuses. He purchased first order lenses for Point Loma, Point Conception, the Farallons, and Cape Disappointment; a second order light for Point Pinos; and a third order light for Humboldt Harbor.

Bartlett reported the costs of first and third orders in the Fresnel system as follows:

	FIRST ORDER	THIRD ORDER
Lens	$ 6,000	$1,600
Lamps (3)	$ 400	$ 250
Frame and extra pieces	$ 750	$ 260
Lantern and extra pieces	$ 4,000	$1,760
Total	$11,150	$3,810

The first two lenses—for Fort Point and Alcatraz—arrived in New York in April 1853 and were immediately transhipped to San Francisco. They arrived there around the first of October. The other lanterns and lenses did not arrive until more than a year later. The first order Point Loma lens and the third order Humboldt Harbor lens did not arrive until early 1855.

There was a question about who would install the expensive new Fresnel system in the Pacific Coast lighthouses. For a time the collector in San Francisco thought the contract required Gibbons and Kelly to furnish "artisans" to put up the illuminating equipment. But due to the delicacy of the new system and concern that the contractors would send inexperienced workmen who might damage the equipment, the collector recommended installing the illuminating apparatuses under separate contracts, using local craftsmen. The lighthouse inspector for the West Coast, Capt. Henry W. Halleck, and the Lighthouse Board concurred. Thus, Gibbons and Kelly were relieved of responsibility for installing the illuminating apparatus.

OPPOSITE:
Craftsmen installed a third order, fixed light lens at Point Loma in 1855. Made in Paris, it stood more than five feet high and three feet wide. In the center, a lamp with three circular wicks, one inside the other, produced a flame of 158 candlepower. The finely ground and highly polished prisms and bull's-eyes that encircled the lens captured the light from this flame, focused and magnified it to about 19,000 candlepower, and sent it out in a horizontal sheet of light.

According to an 1862 directory of lights, the lens at Point Loma "illuminates the entire horizon, and in clear weather should be visible from a mast height of 20 feet above the sea, at a distance of 28 miles."

FUELING THE LIGHTS

For many years the lamps in American lighthouses burned sperm whale oil. In the early 1840s, however, the supply of sperm whale oil began to diminish while at the same time its use for manufacturing purposes increased. The result was a steady rise in price. By 1854 sperm whale oil brought $1.38 per gallon, compared to $.55 per gallon a decade earlier. The Lighthouse Board began to look for a substitute fuel.

While in France contracting for the Fresnel lenses in 1852, Lieutenant Bartlett gathered information on colza, or rapeseed, oil as a possible illuminant. Subsequent tests by the Lighthouse Board showed that colza oil was ideally suited for lighthouse purposes. It was as good as sperm whale oil at half the price. By the late 1850s colza oil was in use in United States lighthouses. Records show that 12,000 gallons of colza oil were purchased in 1862, compared to 5,000 gallons the previous year, indicating the rapid increase in colza oil use. However, not enough rape, the wild cabbage from which rapeseed was obtained, was grown in the United States to supply the needs of the lighthouse system, and farmers did not seem interested in growing the crop for such a limited market.

The Lighthouse Board next considered lard oil. Joseph Henry, secretary of the Smithsonian Institution and chairman of the Committee on Experiments, personally conducted experiments with

From the early 1850s to the late 1880s, shore whalers sailed out of San Diego Harbor to the far side of the kelp beds to wait for migrating gray whales to swim by. As the telltale spout gave away a whale's location, the men sprang into action. Straining with each stroke of the oars, they pulled up alongside so the man in the bow could sink his harpoon into the whale.

They towed the dead whale back to Ballast Point, stripped the blubber from the carcass, and boiled it down for oil. Contrary to some reports, the oil from the shore whaling establishments at Ballast Point was never used in the Point Loma lighthouse. The Lighthouse Board purchased all the oil for the lighthouses under one contract, and it was oil from the sperm whale, not the Pacific gray whale that fueled the lights.

lard oil and reported that he found it to be highly satisfactory in the Fresnel apparatus and in the Franklin lamp "in which the combustion is carried on at a high temperature . . . ." Moreover, lard oil yielded more light than whale oil. As a result of Henry's report, lard oil supplanted sperm whale oil by 1867 as the principal illuminant in lighthouses. Colza oil continued to be used in smaller lamps.

In the 1870s, experiments with kerosene, a mineral oil refined from petroleum, showed it to be a satisfactory fuel. Kerosene was put into use at Point Loma in 1882, and by 1885 kerosene was in general use in U.S. lighthouses. Varieties of refined petroleum remained the principal illuminant in most West Coast lighthouses until the 1920s. The new Point Loma lighthouse used kerosene until it converted to electricity in 1926.

COMPLETING THE POINT LOMA LIGHT

I t is not surprising that the administrative changes in the country's aids to navigation led to some confusion in establishing the new lighthouses. All lights on the California and Oregon coasts were "under the special direction of the Secretary of the Treasury until transferred, December 22, 1852, to the Lighthouse Board," which had been established just two months earlier. Partially due to this administrative limbo and partially due to the conversion to the Fresnel lens system, there was confusion about the order, or size, of some of these early lights.

Point Loma ended up with a third order lens, although early documents refer to a first order system for that light. A. D. Bache, as superintendent of the U.S. Coast Survey, recommended a first class seacoast light for Point Loma. He made his recommendation in 1851, prior to the advent of the Lighthouse Board, so he probably meant the Argand lamp and parabolic reflector. The contract let for building the eight West Coast lighthouses at first called for the illuminating apparatuses to be lamps and reflectors. When it was later decided to install the Fresnel system, the Lighthouse Board, perhaps equating the two systems, contracted with L. Sautter in Paris to provide a first order lens for Point Loma.

*T*he earliest known photograph of the Old Point Loma Lighthouse is circa 1870.

Following the construction of the lighthouses the actual lighting moved very slowly. Much of the delay was due to getting the Fresnel lenses from France. But an important and complicating factor was the apparent ineptitude or lack of interest on the part of the first and second lighthouse inspectors assigned to the Pacific Coast. The third inspector, however, was competent, energetic, and knowledgeable. Maj. Hartman Bache, the uncle of A.D. Bache, transferred from a lighthouse district on the East Coast. To him goes much of the credit for getting the West Coast lighted.

Shortly after Bache arrived on the Pacific Coast on June 30, 1855, he began to take action. He decided to make the Point Loma lighthouse a third order instead of a first order light. The tower was only large enough to support a third order apparatus and that size was sufficient for the purpose. Furthermore, experiments conducted by Fresnel indicated that his third order lens was better than a first-class reflector system. Toward the end of July, Samuel Franklin was dispatched southward with the third order lantern and lens originally intended for Humboldt Harbor. He was instructed to make any changes necessary in the Point Loma tower to receive the lantern. Joseph Smith, apparently a mason, accompanied Franklin.

On August 11, 1855, the San Diego *Herald* announced:

The Schr. Gen. Pierce, *Capt. Badger, which arrived on Friday morning last (Aug. 3), brought down the lantern and other fixtures for the Lighthouse on Point Loma, which will be put up immediately, under the superintendency of Messrs. Smith and Franklin, who came as passengers on the schooner for that purpose. Although the work will be commenced at once, we understand that it will require some two or three months for its completion, on account of the alterations and repairs necessary to be made on the house. We may expect to see the light in operation about the first of November.*

Major Bache visited Point Loma on September 5 and reported:

The coping course of stone had been removed, and, after raising the tower two bricks in height, to give the domical arch sufficient thickness, were replaced, and cramped with iron. The holes for the uprights of the lantern, and the channels for the brackets of the gallery, had been cut to receive them. The sleeping drum and iron manhole, to replace the one of wood, deficient in size, were also set in the domical arch—the top of which was leveled off and well coated with cement. The lantern and lighting apparatus, which had reached the lighthouse, with slight

Major Hartman Bache, engineer, artist, historian, and inspector for the 12th Lighthouse District. He is credited with getting the Pacific Coast lighthouses into service.

exceptions, in perfect order, were in course of cleaning, preparatory to putting up. The dwelling is of stone, and, with the exception of the mortar, which is very bad, is quite a creditable piece of work. The tower is of brick. The mortar is not only bad, but the brick itself of such poor quality, that in places they have wasted away to a depth of a quarter of an inch to two inches. The pointing, both in the dwelling and that part of the tower exposed to the weather is entirely gone. Directed the deficient bricks in the tower cut out and replaced by good ones, and then so much of it as rises above the roof of the dwelling, as well as the brick eaves of the latter, plastered or rough-cast with cement; also the stone work of the dwelling pointed anew.

Bache also ordered the cistern, which had been reported as not holding water, to be "raised by laying a pavement of brick in cement, and then coating the entire interior with the same material." The cistern would hold only 1,240 gallons—a quantity wholly inadequate to supply the lighthouse keepers for a year. As a temporary expedient Bache suggested using casks to hold extra water, "leaving the question of an additional cistern for future consideration." He also ordered the tin roof of the dwelling painted red.

This stereograph by Eadweard Muybridge shows the original sandstone building and brick tower. To slow deterioration caused by exposure to the wind, the tower was plastered over in 1855. In 1879 the south and west walls were coated in cement and painted stone color. The building was painted white in 1887.

965—Point Loma, Light-house, Third Order Fixed Light, 492 feet above the Sea.

Bricks to repair the tower were purchased locally from Thomas Whaley's brickyard at La Playa. Harvey Ladd, who had come to San Diego with the Mormon Battalion, was hired as a mason. Work progressed well, and about the first of October Franklin left for Point

Conception to install the lantern there. Joseph Smith stayed at Point Loma to complete the work and instruct the keepers in how to operate the illuminating apparatus.

When the work concluded, the San Diego *Herald* wrote: "Those employed in putting up the light deserve credit for the manner in which the work has been accomplished and the short time occupied in doing it."

Major Bache ordered James Keating, the first keeper at Point Loma, to display the light on November 15, just 10 days short of a year after the *Herald* had complained about the slowness of getting a light "for the little stack of brick on Point Loma."

Using the small hand lamp called a "lucerne," the light keeper lit the concentric wicks of the large lamp at 15 minutes before sunset on November 15, 1855, and the Point Loma lighthouse blinked to life for the first time. As the night blotted out the day the soft golden glow became more prominent, and the people of San Diego saw for the first time what they would see every night, except in times of fog, for the next 36 years.

Reports from ship captains erased any doubt that remained about the adequacy of a third order Fresnel light as a coast light. Two weeks after the Point Loma light was first exhibited a captain reported to Major Bache that he had seen the light at more than 25 miles. Three months later the skipper of *Golden Gate* said he saw the light at 39 miles.

Major Bache continued to order improvements. He recommended building another road from La Playa to the lighthouse to facilitate the hauling of supplies and, at times, water from La Playa to the site. The road was constructed in fiscal year 1857 for $1,500. It took a different course from the road built by the original contractors. The former ran from Ballast Point in a zig-zag fashion up to the crest of Point Loma at a place almost even with Ballast Point. The La Playa road ran back from the lighthouse along the crest of Point Loma for about two miles and then began a straight, gradual descent to La Playa.

In 1855 the skipper of the U.S. steamer Golden Gate *reported seeing the light from Point Loma at 39 miles. A year before the lighthouse was operational, the* Golden Gate *went aground at Point Loma. The career of this unlucky vessel ended in 1862 when an engine-room fire caused the ship to sink with more than 200 people and a cargo that included $1.4 million in gold coin.*

LIGHTHOUSE KEEPING

Securing personnel to tend the aids to navigation was no easy task; holding them once they were hired was even harder. Low pay was usually the problem.

In the beginning of the lighthouse service, a first order light rated a principal keeper and two assistants; second and third order lights called for a principal keeper and one assistant; fourth and fifth order lights had only a principal keeper. Regardless of order of light, principal keepers received $1,000 annual salary; first assistant keepers received $650; and second assistant keepers, $500. Everyone, from the keepers up to the Lighthouse Board itself, considered the pay inadequate.

Keepers were usually appointed about the time the individual lighthouses were completed. But as was the case at Point Loma, there could be a considerable lag between completion of the lighthouse and installation of the illuminating apparatus to begin operation.

Confusion over the size of the light at Point Loma affected the personnel allowance. Initially the Point Loma lighthouse was to have a light of the first order. About six months after the structure was completed, a principal keeper and two assistants were hired. But when the light was changed to one of the third order, there was also a reduction in personnel allowance. Both assistants were retained until January 1, 1856, when the second assistant tendered his resignation. He gave no reason for leaving, but low pay and effective date of employment were likely factors. With his departure the position of second assistant was discontinued at Point Loma.

The first assistant keeper at the time, George Tolman, was upset

David Splaine, in uniform, plays horseshoes at Ballast Point, where he was the principal keeper after serving as assistant keeper at several other locations.

KEEPERS AND ASSISTANT KEEPERS AT THE OLD POINT LOMA LIGHTHOUSE

Two women served as assistant keepers at the Old Point Loma Lighthouse. Lighthouse keeping was one of the first non-clerical federal occupations open to women, beginning as early as the American Revolution. Many women served with distinction as keepers and assistant keepers when there were few employment opportunities for women other than nursing and teaching.

KEEPERS	DATE APPOINTED	DATE VACATED	SALARY	REMARKS
James P. Keating	Dec. 28, 1854	Feb. 1, 1859	$1,000	Removed
W.C. Wiley	Feb. 1, 1859		1,000	Salary reduced to $800 on Sept. 1, 1859
J.N. Covarrubias	Oct. 9, 1859	Mar. 13, 1860	800	Resigned
Joseph Reiner	Mar. 13, 1860	Nov. 16, 1860	800	Resigned
James P. Keating	Nov. 16, 1860		800	Resigned
W.C. Price	Feb. 16, 1861	Nov. 23, 1867	1,000	
J.D. Jenkins	Nov. 23, 1867	Apr. 24, 1871	1,000	Removed
Isaac Swain	Apr. 24, 1871	May 20, 1871	1,000	Declined
Enos A. Wall	May 20, 1871			
James J. Ferree	Mar. 5, 1872	June 27, 1873	1,000	Resigned
Robert D. Israel	June 27, 1873	Mar. 23, 1891	1,000	Salary reduced to $800 on Jan. 1, 1880; transferred to new Point Loma Light when old lighthouse closed

ASSISTANT KEEPERS	DATE APPOINTED	DATE VACATED	SALARY	REMARKS
George B. Tolman	Jan. 29, 1855	Jan. 29, 1856	$ 650	Resigned
Anthony Genan	Jan. 29, 1855	Jan. 17, 1856	500	2nd assistant position discontinued
Julius Semen	Apr. 28, 1856		650	Salary reduced to $500 on Sept. 1, 1859
W.C. Price			500	Resigned
Thomas Susk	Dec. 6, 1859	Dec. 31, 1859	500	Resigned
J.J. Serano	Dec. 30, 1859	Mar. 13, 1860	500	
W.C. Price	Mar. 13, 1860		500	
S. Fields	Feb. 16, 1861		500	
Christopher P. McAleer	Mar. 7, 1865		625	
Lewis McCoy	Feb. 5, 1867	Nov. 23, 1867	600	Resigned
Eliza Jenkins	Nov. 23, 1867	May 20, 1871	600	Removed
Robert D. Israel	May 20, 1871	June 27, 1873	600	Promoted
Mary [sic] A. Israel	June 27, 1873	Feb. 15, 1876	625	Removed
A.G. Walker	Feb. 15, 1876	May 19, 1876	625	Transferred
J.S. Craig	May 19, 1876	Aug. 13, 1877	625	Resigned
John Stone	Aug. 13, 1877	July 30, 1881	625	Salary reduced to $600 on Jan. 18, 1880 Resigned
Victor H. Richet	July 30, 1881	Nov. 14, 1883	600	Resigned
James Maloney	Nov. 14, 1883	Sept. 15, 1884	600	Resigned
Philip Savage	Sept. 15, 1884	Aug. 14, 1886	600	Resigned
*David R. Splaine	Aug. 14, 1886	Apr. 15, 1889	600	Transferred
Thomas W. Anderson	July 15, 1889	Oct. 25, 1891	600	Resigned
Haydon B. Cartwell	Oct. 28, 1891	Feb. 23, 1894	600	Resigned

The above list was compiled from the following records of the National Archives:
"Record of Lights, Keeper's Names, &c" v.1
"Record of Lights, Keeper's Names, Birthplace, Whence Appointed, Annual Salary, &c." v. 1A, 1853-1870
"Lighthouse Appointments, 1843-1880, Treasury Department," v.2
"Keepers of Light Stations, 1864-1886, no. 3, Division of Appointments, Secretary of the Treasury."
"Keepers of Light Stations, Dist. 5-13, 1862-1900, Division of Appointments, Secretary of the Treasury."
"Keepers of Light Stations, Divisions of Appointments, Office of the Secretary of the Treasury," Series V, v. 6.

*Appointed first keeper of Ballast Point Light on December 1, 1894.

about the effective date of his employment. Tolman had been in the army and served in the Yuma-San Diego area. Upon discharge he settled in San Diego and on January 29, 1855, was appointed first assistant keeper at the Point Loma lighthouse. In the latter part of November he found out that his salary would begin on the day the lighthouse was put into operation—November 15, 1855—and was *not* retroactive to his date of appointment. He wrote directly to Lt. Edmund Hardcastle, secretary of the Lighthouse Board, expressing his displeasure. He identified himself as having served a few years before in the same regiment with Hardcastle in the New River area east of San Diego. Tolman said he understood that his pay was to begin on the date of appointment, and on that basis he had in the meantime run up a sizable boarding bill. It is unlikely Tolman received back pay. He resigned his assistant keeper's job on January 29, 1856, the first anniversary of his appointment.

Not only was turnover a problem in filling the low-paying assistant keeper positions, but also the men attracted to these jobs sometimes came from the fringes of society. Four months after the lighting of Point Loma, keeper James Keating complained: "I have been unfortunate in respect of assistants. There comes a strange one every month."

Principal keepers tended to remain longer than assistant keepers. During the 36 years of operation of the light on Point Loma, there were 11 keepers and 22 assistants. The last keeper, Robert D. Israel, was on duty for 18 years at the Point Loma lighthouse. He transferred to the new lighthouse when it began operating, where he served another year.

The principal keeper was usually nominated for the position by the local collector of customs. If the Lighthouse Board endorsed the nominee, an official appointment was made by the Secretary of the Treasury. By the 1890s operating procedures required the light keeper to be on duty for three months and then pass an examination given by the district inspector before being certified to the Lighthouse Board for a full appointment.

As time went on, the lighthouse jobs took on the form of a career service. Toward the end of the 19th century transfers of personnel between lighthouses began to occur, and keepers were appointed from the ranks of assistant keepers. For example, David Splaine served as assistant keeper in several lighthouses on the Pacific Coast, including the one on Point Loma. By the time the new lighthouse was established at Ballast Point he had gained enough experience to be appointed its first keeper.

By the late 19th century, lighthouse keeping had become a career service. David Splaine (background) and Robert Israel (foreground) first served as assistant keepers before moving into positions as principal keepers.

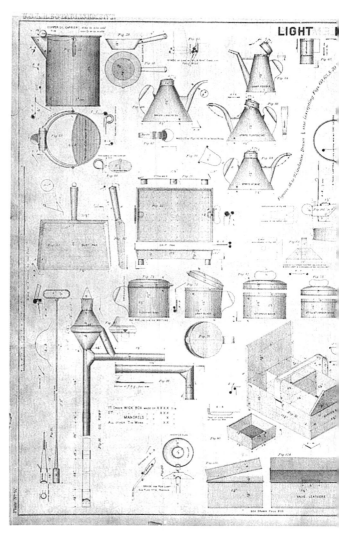

DUTIES OF THE KEEPERS   The principal task of the keepers was to keep the light burning brightly from sunset to sunrise. Round-the-clock attention, seven days a week, required dedication. The work itself was not difficult physically, and operating a lighthouse required no great amount of imagination, provided one could read. In justifying higher pay for keepers in order to attract more literate candidates, the Lighthouse Board noted that there were ample instructions to guide the keepers if they could but understand them. The principal keeper of the Point Loma lighthouse had copies of *Lighthouse Establishment Instructions* and *Instructions and Directions for the Management of Lenses, Lights and Beacons*, as well as a copy of the current *Light List*.

Other publications available to the keeper included: *List of Illuminating Apparatuses, Fixtures, Implements, Tools, Miscellaneous Articles, and Supplies in General Use in the U.S. Lighthouses, Lighted-*

The Lighthouse Board provided keepers with an assortment of implements to care for the lamps and lenses, plus detailed instructions on their use. Equipment included, for example, feather dusters to dust the lens without scratching; large copper oil carriers to bring oil from the basement to fill smaller lamp feeders, and trimmers to keep wicks at a prescribed height.

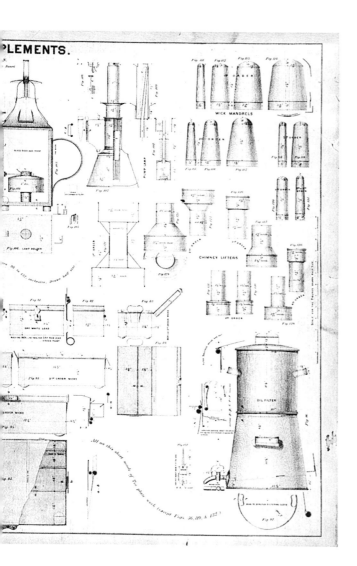

PLEMENTS.

WICK MANDRELS

CHIMNEY LIFTERS

OIL FILTER

The keepers climbed to the tower many times a day to keep the lantern lit and in good repair.

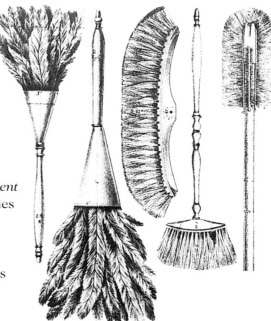

Beacons, and Light Vessels . . . ; Instructions and Directions to Guide Light-House Keepers and Others Belonging to the Lighthouse Establishment; and *Management of Lens Apparatus and Lamps.* In his administrative duties the keeper could also draw upon the *List of Placards, Blank Forms, Circulars, Pamphlets, and Books.*

Printed instructions spelled out the routine of a keeper's job, such as alternating the lamps inside the lens every 15 days, washing the lens every two months with spirits of wine, and polishing it annually with rouge. Any questions about the work could be answered by carefully perusing the instructions available. If a keeper dropped oil on the lens, instructions told him to use spirits of wine in cleaning it off. If he did not know how to trim a wick or adjust a lamp, a step-by-step detailed description was available, including a picture of what the

The schooner Loma, *launched on August 13, 1857, from James Keating's shipyard, was the first vessel built on San Diego Bay. This photo shows a similar vessel off Pt. Loma in 1905.*

Regimented daily maintenance assured that the lighting apparatus was always clean and in good repair.

lamp flame should look like. Little was left to the discretion of the keeper. A neat, workable lighthouse could be kept with only a modicum of intelligence, imagination, and physical energy.

Since the work was not too difficult, some lighthouse keepers had outside activities. The first keeper of the Point Loma lighthouse, James Keating, for example, operated a shipyard—San Diego's first—and in 1857 launched the first vessel built in the city. The Lighthouse Board recognized that the keepers might work elsewhere but required that they not carry on any business that kept them away from the lighthouse for a prolonged period of time.

Procedures called for maintaining regular 4-hour watches. To avoid having the less desired watches fall entirely upon one person, the watches were to be alternated daily. In practice, however, this rule was apparently not always followed. At Point Loma the keepers reportedly stood 24-hour watches, changing at midnight.

To perform the main job effectively, lighting equipment had to be in good condition, and the keepers were instructed to have "everything put in order for lighting in the evening by 10 o'clock a.m., daily." Work at light stations with two or more keepers was divided into two "departments." One keeper had to clean and polish the lens, clean and fill the lamp, "remove all dust with the brushes from the frame-work of the apparatus, fit wicks if required, and if not required trim carefully those already fitted to the burner and see that everything connected with the apparatus and lamp is perfectly clean, and the light ready for lighting at the proper time in the evening."

The other keeper had to "clean the plate glass of the lantern inside and outside; clean all the copper and brass work of the apparatus, the utensils used in the lantern and watchroom; the walls, floors, and balconies of the lantern, . . . the tower stairways, landing, doors, windows, window-recesses, and passages from the lantern to the oil cellars." In performing their work in the lantern the keepers were instructed to wear linen aprons to prevent the possibility of their coarse clothes scratching the lens. When the lens was not in use or being worked on, a special linen cover was draped over it to protect it from dust, the sun, and the possibility of it being scratched.

In addition to the routine work of cleaning and lighting the light, the keepers attended to maintenance, which for the most part consisted of repairs of a minor nature to the equipment and structures. Major repairs were normally taken care of through contract and, when necessary, funded by special appropriations from Congress as specifically requested by the Lighthouse Board.

LIGHTHOUSE LIVING   Life at a lighthouse varied somewhat with the peculiarities of its location. At Point Loma, for example, obtaining adequate water was an ongoing problem. For many years the lighthouse had only one cistern—the one in the basement—to hold rainwater run-off from the roof. Because of very low rainfall in the San Diego area, there was often too little run-off to fill the cistern. Consequently, when the keepers ran out of water they had to haul barrels by wagon from the spring at La Playa that was 7 miles away or from a well at Roseville that was 10 miles away. The journey was over roads dotted with chuckholes, and then a steep ascent to the top of Point Loma. The number of trips a year depended upon the annual rainfall. A second cistern was added sometime between 1858 and 1873, but this also could not collect enough water. In 1883 a large concrete catch basin in front of the lighthouse and a third cistern were added, but the problems continued when annual rainfall was not adequate to meet needs.

Aside from dry conditions, weather was not a particular problem at Point Loma. There were occasional squalls, but violent storms were rare. However, on October 2, 1858, a severe gale lashed the San Diego area for six hours. Several ships in the harbor dragged their anchors and were driven aground. A couple of wooden structures in Old San Diego toppled. "So fearful was the gale at Point Loma the Lighthouse keeper, Capt. Keating, was obliged to leave at 12 o'clock M., fearing the tower would fall."

Although the lighthouse was not harmed by that storm, four years later an earthquake did damage the lighthouse. The damage must not have been too severe, however, because the secretary of the Lighthouse Board felt he had authority to order immediate repairs without first consulting the board.

At "unusually isolated" lighthouses, the Lighthouse Board provided each keeper with 200 pounds of pork, 100 pounds of beef, 2 barrels of flour, 50 pounds of rice, 50 pounds of brown sugar, 24 pounds of coffee, 10 gallons of beans or peas, 4 gallons of vinegar,

Lack of water was an ongoing concern on the windswept heights of Point Loma. Over time, large catch basins and cisterns were added to collect rainwater. Still, keepers sometimes had to haul barrels of water by wagon from wells several miles away. One of the three original cisterns remains.

and 2 barrels of potatoes a year. Where feasible, lighthouse keepers had gardens. At Point Loma a potato patch was maintained just north of the lighthouse and later moved to a 1½-acre site near the present U.S.S. Bennington Monument in Fort Rosecrans National Cemetery. The patch contained only potatoes; lack of water prevented growing anything else. The last keeper's wife, Maria Israel, managed to keep a tomato vine growing and bearing year after year by careful nursing and protection.

The lighthouse was often visited by local residents. Sometimes they came to watch the shore whalers from Ballast Point harpoon migrating Pacific gray whales just beyond the kelp beds off Point Loma. Groups of young people packed picnic lunches and journeyed to the lighthouse for pleasant outings. There was at least one instance of the lighthouse barn being used for a dance by the local young people.

In 1874, a reporter for the *San Diego Union* wrote this account of the station:

The lighthouse was always a popular destination for sightseers and picnickers. Then, as now, people were attracted to the superior views. This 1890s photo shows early evidence of neglect after the lighthouse was abandoned in 1891.

The lighthouse upon the extreme point of Point Loma is some fourteen miles from San Diego and is approached by one of the most beautiful drives in the world, to those who enjoy the cool, bracing breezes. . . . The buildings consist of a very neat and commodious dwelling house surmounted by a tower fifteen feet high, also several immense sheds erected by the government for the purpose of catching rainwater enough during the rainy season to fill the cistern. These roofs are very flat and are arranged with spouts, etc. Water and wood are items of considerable importance here, both having heretofore been brought from San Diego. We were conducted through the entire establishment by the gentlemanly keeper, Mr. Israel, and his wife, who is his assistant in the care of the light, which is very ingenious. Everything is scrupulously clean; the glass reflectors of the lantern fairly dazzle the eyes. There is a small room in the tower, below the light, for the accommodation of the watchers, and here they pass the long hours of the night, watching alternately the light of the huge lantern, which is a welcome beacon to the "toilers of the sea" who may be within reach of its rays. The light, which is 480 [actually 462] feet above the ocean can be seen upon clear nights a distance of sixteen or eighteen miles. The roar of the wind about the tower is almost deafening, and necessitates the voice being raised to the highest pitch whilst conversing within.

The vegetation around the lighthouse is very meagre, consisting of a very low, scrubby sage brush. Mrs. Israel told us that she had endeavored in vain to make a few of the most hardy flowers and vegetables grow, but the position was too much exposed to admit cultivation. . . .

Normally, supplies such as oil, wicks, mops, brooms, and equipment were delivered to lighthouses quarterly. The procedure described for a New England lighthouse in the 1890s was probably duplicated on the Pacific Coast. On arriving at a light station the supply vessel anchored and a party landed and made its way to the lighthouse. After a brief social period and exchange of pleasantries the keeper produced his worn out brushes, mops and brooms, broken tools, and decrepit lamps, to be exchanged for new ones. The old items were taken back to the vessel, and when the ship was far out at sea were dumped overboard. The captain of the supply vessel did not want them to be washed ashore to be again offered in evidence.

Probably in the 1880s, certainly prior to 1890, the Lighthouse Board began supplying portable libraries to the keepers. The books were arranged in cases that "make rather a neat appearance when set upright on a table, and they only need be closed and locked to be ready for transportation." Each contained about 50 volumes of a mixture of historical and scientific books, poetry, novels, and a Bible and a prayer book. The libraries were usually exchanged at the quarterly inspection.

Uniforms for the light keepers were also introduced in the 1880s. Dress and fatigue uniforms were prescribed in 1883, and the following year the Lighthouse Board put the regulations into effect, giving the first uniform free to each keeper. The uniform consisted of trousers, vest, and a double-breasted coat of dark indigo blue jersey or flannel. The coat had five large yellow metal buttons on each side. The cap was of cloth with a visor and a yellow lighthouse badge on the front of the cap.

Lighthouse keepers wore civilian clothes until the Lighthouse Board issued official uniforms in 1884. The men's uniforms consisted of dark indigo-blue jersey or flannel coat, vest, trousers, and cap or helmet. (Women were not required to wear uniforms.) Numbers on the emblems indicated the keeper's rank: "K" is the chief keeper; "2" is the second assistant keeper.

"U.S.L.H.E." stands for the United States Light House Establishment, the body created in 1789 to manage the nation's lighthouses. It became the U.S. Light House Service in 1910 and was transferred to the U.S. Coast Guard in 1939.

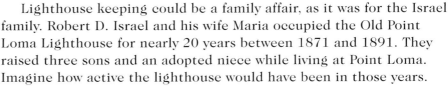

Lighthouse keeping could be a family affair, as it was for the Israel family. Robert D. Israel and his wife Maria occupied the Old Point Loma Lighthouse for nearly 20 years between 1871 and 1891. They raised three sons and an adopted niece while living at Point Loma. Imagine how active the lighthouse would have been in those years.

Robert Decatur Israel, the best known of the keepers at the Old Point Loma Lighthouse, was born in Pittsburgh, Pennsylvania, on March 23, 1826. He was a chairmaker by trade, but as a young man he joined the U.S. Army. He reportedly stormed Chapultepec Castle with General Winfield Scott during the Mexican-American War. In 1849, after being mustered out of the army, he came to San Diego. At that time San Diego was just a small town of about 650 residents, and he soon became an active member of the community.

Israel's early career was a mixture of private jobs and public offices. In the early 1850s he was a policeman and jailer. In 1851, he joined Fitzgerald's Volunteers, commanded by Major G. B. Fitzgerald, U.S. Army. They set out to subdue Antonio Garra and his followers who were trying to regain land settled by Americans. Garra was later captured by Indians loyal to the Americans and sent to San Diego where he was tried and found guilty. Israel was in charge of the execution, and on January 10, 1852, gave the order for the firing squad to shoot Garra.

That same year, at the age of 26, Israel married into one of San Diego's most prominent families. His bride was Maria Arcadia Alipás, the 16-year-old granddaughter of Juan Machado, reportedly one of the earliest settlers of San Diego. Maria's mother was Juana de Dios Machado de Alipás, and her father was Damasio Alipás. Alipás died in Mexico, and Juana married Thomas Wrightington, one of the first Americans to settle in San Diego.

Robert and Maria had four sons: Henry Clay, born February 11, 1862; Joseph Perry, born February 3, 1865 (died in 1869 before the family moved to the lighthouse); Robert Lincoln, born July 8, 1867; and a second Joseph Perry, born June 12, 1871. Shortly before the last child was born, Israel was appointed assistant keeper at the Point Loma lighthouse.

Robert's marriage to Maria established him socially in San Diego, and his many jobs and offices established him as a member of the business community. In partnership with John I. Van Alst, he was a blacksmith and carriage maker, and with his brother Joseph, a contractor. In 1858, he was a justice of the peace,

Maria Israel, a descendant of one of San Diego's earliest Mexican settlers, married Robert Israel in 1852. Interracial marriage and ethnic assimilation were common in southern California. Hard working and talented, Maria raised a family, attended to household chores, and for nearly three years served as assistant keeper at the Old Point Loma Lighthouse. In her "spare" time, she fashioned intricate framed floral designs from bits of chiton and abalone shell to sell to visitors.

and in 1865, a school trustee. The census records for 1860 list his occupation as a farmer. He had 80 acres of improved land and 80 acres of unimproved land, together with five horses, three milk cows, three mules, and $500 worth of farm machinery. The cash value of his farm was listed at $1,000.

In the 1800s the job of lighthouse keeper was generally a political appointment. Prospective keepers were nominated for the position by the local collector of the port, or customs official. The Lighthouse Board either endorsed or rejected the nomination, with the Secretary of the Treasury officially appointing the keeper.

On May 20, 1871, Robert Israel was appointed assistant keeper for the Point Loma lighthouse at a salary of $600 a year. Israel was nominated by his wife's cousin's husband, Dr. David B. Hoffman.

Mr. and Mrs. Robert D. Israel and grandchildren, photographed in Coronado shortly before Robert's death in 1908.

Hoffman was collector of the port of San Diego from 1869 to 1872. He was also married to Maria Delores Wilder, the daughter of Peter Wilder and Guadalupe Machado, an aunt of Maria Arcadia Alipás Israel. At the same time that Hoffman nominated Israel as assistant keeper, he nominated Enos Wall as principal keeper. Wall was married to Antonia Machado an aunt of Maria Hoffman and Maria Israel.

On June 27, 1873, Israel was appointed the principal keeper at Point Loma. He held the position until the lighthouse went out of service in 1891. During that time, his life apparently centered around his official duties and his family. He watched his boys grow to manhood, and when one of Maria's sisters died, he and Maria took their niece, Emma Minter, into their home. Also one of their grandsons, Robert Davis "Bert" Israel, the son of Robert Lincoln Israel, was born in the lighthouse in 1888.

Maria Israel presumably stayed busy raising the boys, and for three years she also served as assistant keeper. It is not known whether her husband made her stand her regular watch at night or not. Some say he did and that Mrs. Israel whiled away her watch-hours knitting. She would sit in her rocker on the first floor as near the stairwell as possible. A circular hole in the deck of the tower permitted the light from the lamp inside the lens to beam downward, providing just the light Mrs. Israel needed to do her knitting.

Mrs. Israel turned her hand to other decorative artwork as well. With various small shells her children collected from the tidepool area below

Robert's skill as a chairmaker was no doubt reflected in the furnishings of the Israels' home. However, after they left Point Loma, a fire destroyed their house near Escondido, with almost all of their furniture. Today, the lighthouse has a few items that belonged to the Israels, including examples of Maria's shell art, but most of the furnishings are period pieces not original to their home. The parlor (above) and master bedroom represent the lifestyle of lighthouse keepers, 1887–1891.

the lighthouse she made beautiful and intricate floral designs. These designs were placed in heavy wooden frames which were decorated principally with chiton shells and fragments of abalone shells. She sometimes sold her artwork to lighthouse visitors.

Abalone shells, with their varicolored pearl-like interiors, could be shaped into a great variety of attractive adornments. One of the assistant keepers, David Splaine, carved buttons for his little daughter's topcoat from the shells; two of these buttons are in the museum collection at Cabrillo National Monument.

When the old lighthouse was replaced by a new one at the ocean's edge in 1891, the Israels moved to the new location. Robert was keeper at the new lighthouse for nearly a year before resigning. Apparently, a dispute with the Lighthouse Board over the lack of fresh water led to Israel's departure. By then he was sixty-six and, perhaps, tiring of his long career. He and Maria moved to Coronado, where he died in 1908. As a veteran of the Mexican War, Israel was buried in what was then called the Fort Rosecrans Post Cemetery, just north of Cabrillo National Monument.

THE CHANGING CHARACTER OF POINT LOMA

As was the case with other light stations along the Pacific Coast, the original dwelling and tower at Point Loma eventually became inadequate for the necessities of an active station. Barns, sheds, and other buildings were later added.

Family living quarters were cramped. In the 1870s two rooms were fitted up in a portion of the wood and oil storehouse as a dwelling for the assistant keeper. This shed was built of rough unseasoned lumber and was lined inside with cloth and paper. Later the inside walls were lined with tongue and groove boards, but in 1877 it was still described as unfit for quarters. How long this building served as a dwelling for the assistant keeper is not known, but additional work was done in 1886.

Other buildings were added from time to time. A barn was constructed near the lighthouse in 1875. In 1881 a boathouse was built at Ballast Point to house the lighthouse boat which had been acquired in 1868. A winch for hauling up the boat was also installed at that time.

The lighthouse structure was unpainted until 1879 when there was concern that exposure to the weather was deteriorating the soft sandstone. The west side and south end walls were covered with a heavy coat of Portland cement mortar and then painted with two coats of stone-color paint.

Over the years the *Light Lists* described the Point Loma lighthouse variously as gray and yellow sandstone and from 1855 to 1877 having a red lantern. The *Light List* for 1888 describes it as white for the first time, stating: "Low white tower, rising from white dwelling, lantern black." Thus the lighthouse was not painted the "traditional" white until 1887.

For its first 34 years the Old Point Loma Lighthouse exhibited a fixed white light beaming in all directions, until

*P*lan of the lighthouse complex in 1881.

KEEPER'S DWELLING, TOWER, AND OUT-HOUSES
ON A SCALE OF
1 : 396.

*S*everal outbuildings were added over the years. This photo, circa 1887–1891, shows the assistant keeper's quarters, barn, and the lighthouse painted white.

the Lighthouse Board determined that the light could be confused with other lights along the coast. On April 1, 1889, the characteristic of the Point Loma light changed to "fixed white, varied by flashes, alternately red and white, interval between flashes one minute."

Normally a flashing characteristic in a Fresnel lens is obtained by rotating the lens. But the Point Loma lens had not been designed to rotate; it was fixed in place. Conceivably the lens could have been redesigned to rotate, or the old lens could have been replaced with one that rotated. But either modifying or exchanging the lens would have taken the lighthouse out of service for an extended time. There is no historical evidence that this occurred. Instead, a rotating red shield was placed inside the lens. Many of the early Fresnel lenses were designed by the manufacturer to flash. These used a shield— some a solid shield that blanked out the light to obtain a simple flashing characteristic; and some a red shield to obtain a flashing red and white effect.

The flashing red and white light continued to be the distinguishing characteristic of the Point Loma lighthouse even after it moved to the ocean's edge. It is interesting to note that when the lens was made for the new lighthouse certain panels of the lens were made with red glass. But the new lens was never used at Point Loma. It was such a work of art that it was displayed at the Paris Exhibition where it won a prize. The lens also won a medal at the Columbia Exposition in Chicago. By the time the Exposition was over, the new Point Loma lighthouse already had a lens and the prize-winning one originally ordered for Point Loma was sent to the Chicago Harbor lighthouse instead.

At about the same time that the characteristic of the Old Point Loma light was changed, Captain Israel, then the keeper, reported receiving orders to reduce the lamp from three concentric wicks to two. This maneuver saved half a gallon of fuel a night. Kerosene was then selling for 14 cents a gallon, which meant the Federal Government saved only $25 a year in fuel at the Point Loma light. Eliminating the wick cut the light's candlepower from 158 to 73, endangering ships and sailors at sea. A disgusted Captain Israel complained that the light could barely be seen. How long the order remained in force is not known.

THE OLD LIGHT GOES OUT

Fog was a problem for the Point Loma lighthouse almost from the start. Because of its height—it was the highest lighthouse in the United States at the time—the light was often obscured by high fog, while the rest of the coastline was distinctly visible. It was of little practical value as an aid to navigation during those times. Plans to move the light began in earnest in the late 1880s. A new site was selected on Pelican Point at the tip of Point Loma some 30 feet above the sea—about 400 feet lower than the old lighthouse.

The U.S. Army controlled all of the land on Point Loma except for the lighthouse reservation. In 1882 the Secretary of the Treasury applied to the Secretary of War for land to erect two new lighthouses: a coastal light to guide ships along the coast and toward San Diego Harbor and a harbor light to guide ships into the harbor. In 1889 the army transferred the requested land to the Lighthouse Board on the condition that it "be vacated at such time as the needs of [the War] Department require."

Construction of the new coastal lighthouse on Pelican Point began that same year, and most of the buildings were finished by June 1890. The third order lens atop a metal skeleton tower went on for the first time on March 23, 1891. The harbor light was erected at nearby

The frequent fogs that shrouded the lighthouse were a persistent problem, and in 1891 the light atop Point Loma was extinguished. A new Point Loma Light Station went into operation on Pelican Point. Even then, the approach to the harbor could be hazardous. In 1909, heavy seas drove the lumber schooner Alice McDonald *onto rocks near the new light. She lay aground until the crew could unload enough cargo for her to float free.*

ice McDonald, Wrecked off Point Loma. Cal. Dec 31.1909.
Passmore.

Ballast Point, a protrusion of land perpendicular to Point Loma that marks the entrance to the harbor.

Abandoned, the Old Point Loma Lighthouse fell on hard times. Eventually, the outbuildings disappeared, and vandals violated the lighthouse itself, breaking windows and carting away parts of the old building.

By 1910 the wooden lean-to in the back of the old building had fallen away. The large concrete rain catchment basin in the front of the building was still there, but only two large lumps on the edge denoted former cisterns. By 1913, the lantern had been stripped of its glass and roof. That year the commanding officer at Fort Rosecrans recommended that the dilapidated structure be torn down.

After years of honorable service, the lighthouse fell victim to the ravages of time, weather, and vandals. People broke windows, wrote on walls, and used the basement as a comfort station. By 1913 the old lighthouse was in such a state of ruin that the commanding officer at Fort Rosecrans recommended tearing it down.

But the old building was still a favorite tourist spot because of the magnificent view from the tower. The ruins were sometimes called the "Old Spanish Lighthouse," although the reason is unclear. Perhaps the name came about because tiles from the old Spanish Fort Guijarros were used in constructing the building. Another theory is that the keepers married women of Spanish descent and a Spanish air may have prevailed about the place. However, no early visitors to the lighthouse mention any Spanish trappings. Moreover, the grandson of long-time keeper Robert Israel reported that during the years he lived with his grandparents his grandfather discouraged Mrs. Israel from instilling any semblance of her Spanish heritage in the children.

It is more likely that the reference to "Old Spanish Lighthouse" is of 20th-century origin and not from the active years of the structure. In the early 1900s a black guide named Ruben may have coined the name to romanticize the old ruins.

SAVING OLD POINT LOMA LIGHTHOUSE

Vandalism and lack of upkeep took their toll on the "Old Spanish Lighthouse." Army officials considered either tearing down the eyesore or repairing the building and converting it into a military radio station.

Meanwhile, a movement was under way to erect a memorial to Juan Rodríguez Cabrillo, the first European explorer of the west coast of what is now the United States. The Order of Panama, an organization dedicated to commemorating California's Spanish heritage, spearheaded the drive for the memorial and proposed that a statue 150 feet tall be placed "on that noble and commanding cape, Point Loma which is . . . the first land ever seen by a civilized man on the Pacific verge of the United States."

The Order of Panama negotiated with the army for a site for the Cabrillo statue. The first site selected was 300 feet south of the Old Point Loma Lighthouse, but the army had plans for that particular spot and recommended instead the site on which the lighthouse stood. The old abandoned lighthouse would be removed and replaced by the huge statue of Cabrillo. The Cabrillo memorial committee agreed and also consented to letting the army establish its radio station in the pedestal of the statue.

President Woodrow Wilson signed a Proclamation on October 14, 1913, to set aside one-half acre of ground surrounding the Old Point Loma Lighthouse as Cabrillo National Monument and permit the Order of Panama to erect the heroic statue. Anticipating the signing of the proclamation, the Order of Panama had held formal dedication ceremonies at the lighthouse site on the previous September 26.

But by good fortune the Order of Panama never carried through with its plans, and in time the organization dissolved. The old lighthouse survived, part of the newly established national monument and the responsibility of the U.S. War Department.

The Order of Panama, shown below in ceremonial garb, was formed by prominent San Diego businessmen in 1912 to promote the Panama-California Exposition of 1915. It proposed erecting a 150-foot monument on the site of the old lighthouse to honor explorer Juan Rodríguez Cabrillo. Above, sculptor Allen Hutchinson created this miniature model of his concept for the monument. Fortunately, the Order of Panama did not carry out its plan, and the statue that memorializes Cabrillo today differs in scale and setting.

Views of the lighthouse under U.S. Army authority between 1912 and 1935.

In 1915 the army spent $360 to repair the old building and reported that further improvements were contemplated. The army rejected a proposal that the old lighthouse be turned over to the California Federation of Women's Clubs, although the ladies were allowed to place a plaque on the old structure if they desired. Nothing came of that suggestion. In the fall of 1916 the army noted that the old building was one "of considerable historical interest." Because there were no restroom facilities and visitors used "the basement and some of the . . . rooms rendering the building unsanitary," the army recommended that a concrete comfort station be added. Nothing came of that proposal either.

For a time the army encouraged soldiers and their families to live in the old lighthouse, which at least temporarily halted its decline. The army used the building as a radio station from about 1915 to 1920. From 1921 to 1934 the army allowed Mrs. H.E. Cook to live rent-free in the lighthouse to deter vandalism. She made a living selling postcards, curios, and refreshments in the parlor.

But these were temporary uses, and the lighthouse continued its downhill slide. It was a sad and forlorn sight. The commanding officer at Fort Rosecrans, Captain Fenton Jacobs, notified the local Chamber of Commerce that the old building was an eyesore and in danger of being razed. A group from the Chamber tried to raise money from interested citizens by subscription to restore the old lighthouse and beautify the grounds, but like many previous efforts, nothing came of this.

Finally in 1931 the Ninth Army Corps found funds to repair the old lighthouse. Holes in the roof were patched; windows were replaced and protected by iron bars; and the building was painted inside and out.

These repairs were enough to stabilize the lighthouse until 1933 when Cabrillo National Monument was turned over to the National Park Service. An Executive Order signed by President Franklin D. Roosevelt in 1933 took most of the national

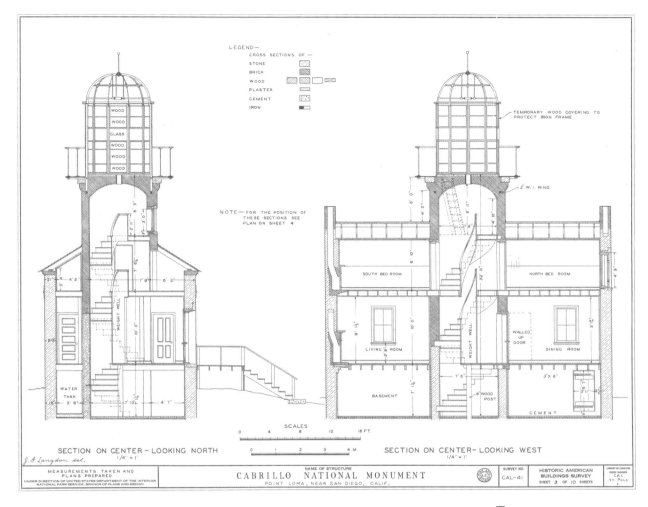

military parks, national battlefield sites, and national monuments
from the jurisdiction of other agencies, including the War
Department, and placed them under the National Park Service.

Upon receiving Cabrillo National Monument, the National Park
Service began to rehabilitate the old lighthouse. First the building
was examined carefully, and detailed drawings were made for the
Historic American Buildings Survey. Architects learned a great deal
from the historical record and from what the building itself revealed.
The National Park Service began to restore the building to what it
believed to be the original condition. It replaced rotten wood, rebuilt
the lean-to, renewed the flooring throughout, and reconstructed the
metal lantern crowning the tower. Some modern concessions were
made for public use, such as adding electrical fixtures and plumbing.
The wooden treads and risers in the tower stairway and the window

*The National Park Service
acquired the lighthouse as
part of Cabrillo National
Monument in 1933.
Systematic rehabilitation
began soon after, starting
with detailed drawings in
1934–1935 for the Historic
American Buildings
Survey.*

From time to time occupants set up sales areas to offer mementos to eager visitors. This 1949 photo shows a gift shop in the parlor of the lighthouse.

sashes and doors were replaced with metal for fire protection. The basement was completely refinished.

The restoration work was completed in 1935. A concessioner, Clifton Rock, who was also custodian of the monument, set up his operation in the lower south room. Rock operated a tea room in the lower north room. He and his wife Mildred also lived in the building.

Many people came to the monument to see the restored lighthouse structure and to climb the tower for the magnificent view. But in 1941 visits to the monument stopped because wartime security precluded non-military activity on Point Loma. The armed forces used the lighthouse during World War II. First the U.S. Navy used it as a signal tower for ships coming to San Diego. If the ship flashed back the correct sign, the huge submarine nets stretching across the entrance to the harbor were pulled aside to admit the vessel. The lighthouse served this purpose for about a year until another tower was built for a signal station just to the south. The old building was then used primarily for storage. The army returned the monument to the National Park Service in 1946, and on November 11, 1946, the public was again welcomed.

A National Park Service inspection in the spring of 1947 recommended a number of repairs to the old lighthouse, including sandblasting the outside of the lantern to remove the army's camouflage paint. Upon completion, the lighthouse, freshly painted white, reopened and resumed its place as the centerpiece of Cabrillo National Monument.

In the years following World War II, the popularity of the lighthouse grew as more and more people explored the rooms and climbed the stairs to the lantern to enjoy the view of San Diego and

4503 Old Spanish Lighthouse, Cabrillo National Monument,

Point Loma, San Diego, California

A souvenir postcard from the 1930s shows the revival of the lighthouse after near extinction. Note the title "Old Spanish Lighthouse," a popular nickname among tourists.

By the 1950s, when this photo was taken, Cabrillo was the most visited national monument in the country. People came from all over the world to see the breathtaking views and the intriguing lighthouse.

the Pacific Ocean. By the mid-1950s Cabrillo National Monument was the most visited national monument in the country, thanks largely to the lighthouse.

The park grew in size as well as popularity. In 1966, the National Park Service added a new visitor center with auditorium, view building, and administrative offices. The lighthouse itself received new attention, too, as the National Park Service determined how best to let the building tell its story. With documented information about actual residents of the Old Point Loma Lighthouse, the National Park Service restored and refurnished the lighthouse to the period when Robert and Maria Israel lived there. It now looks as if the keeper and his wife just stepped out to attend to their chores.

In returning the structure to resemble its 1887–1891 appearance, the National Park Service dismantled the lantern and replaced the deteriorated iron supports, rebuilt portions of the brick tower, replaced the standing-seam metal roof with a more historically accurate wood shingle roof, and installed the correct third order fixed lens in the rebuilt lantern. For the first time in more than 90 years, the outside of the lighthouse looked as it did when it went out of service in 1891.

On the interior, National Park Service historians purchased and installed numerous pieces of late 19th-century furniture, books, photographs, and personal and decorative items throughout the lighthouse, including a few items donated by the Israel family. Artisans installed replica wallpaper and floor coverings in the parlor and bedrooms, and added faux graining to the baseboards, doors, and windows. Now visitors could visualize the keeper writing in the log at the parlor desk while his wife prepared the evening meal in the kitchen.

The restoration has evolved over many years. In 2003 the National Park Service restored the historical setting of the lighthouse by removing an asphalt loop road and parking spaces, restoring walkways, outlining the locations of the barn and oil shed, reconstructing the concrete rain catchment basin, installing a flag pole and picket fence, and rebuilding the assistant keeper's quarters where they had been historically. Exhibits added in 2005 tell the story of the Point Loma lighthouses;

In 1983 the National Park Service rebuilt the tower and the lantern as part of an on-going restoration program.

150TH ANNIVERSARY TRIBUTE

On Sunday, November 13, 2005, fourteen descendants of lighthouse keepers and assistant keepers from the three San Diego lighthouses (Old Point Loma, new Point Loma, and Ballast Point) gathered on the grounds of Cabrillo National Monument to help commemorate the 150th anniversary of the Old Point Loma Lighthouse. Since November 15, 1855, when keeper James P. Keating lit the lamp in the tower for the first time, the venerable lighthouse has stood watch on the cliffs overlooking San Diego Bay and the Pacific Ocean. Although no longer in active service as a lighthouse, it continues to have an important role in portraying the era in America's maritime history when dedicated men and women tended the beacons that guided mariners to safe harbors.

Anniversary events captured the spirit of the active years at Old Point Loma Lighthouse. National Park Service staff and volunteers led living history demonstrations and tours of the restored lighthouse and grounds. Nineteenth-century music, games, and crafts provided a festive setting. The National Park Service showcased a new exhibit on the history and significance of the lighthouses of Point Loma. At the end of the day, the 10-year-old great-great-great granddaughter of Robert and Maria Israel ceremonially lit the lamp in the tower of the Old Point Loma Lighthouse.

the duties and lifestyle of the men and women who kept the light; operation of the lights; and development of the west coast network of lights. The third order flashing lens from the new Point Loma lighthouse is the centerpiece of the exhibit. On loan from the U.S. Coast Guard, it is the lens first lit on March 23, 1891, when the Old Point Loma Lighthouse closed and service began at the new Point Loma Light Station.

Today the restored Old Point Loma Lighthouse at Cabrillo National Monument is a symbol of the first successful efforts to obtain aids to navigation for the West Coast. But more important, as it stands overlooking the beautiful and busy San Diego Harbor, the old lighthouse is a link with the past. The lighthouse represents significant progress toward providing better and more reliable navigational aids to make the mariner's passage safer.

In 1890 Charles Dudley Warner wrote of Point Loma in Harper's New Monthly Magazine: "This site commands one of the most remarkable views on the accessible world, one of the three or four really great prospects which the traveler can recall, astonishing in its immensity, interesting in its peculiar details. It is one of the loveliest prospects in the world, and worth long travel to see,…"

Since 1933 the National Park Service has worked to preserve, restore, and interpret the irreplaceable resources of the Old Point Loma Lighthouse and the surrounding coastal Mediterranean habitat for this and future generations to enjoy.

ACKNOWLEDGEMENTS

Cabrillo National Monument Foundation expresses its deep gratitude to the following major donors and others who made this book possible.

Dr. James Nauman
The Beth V. Paynter Memorial Fund
Carolyn M. Medina in memory of Joe M. Medina, Jr.

Dr. John and Dulie Ahlering

David and Ceil Ball

The Black

Richard Brown

Ian Campbell

Betsey and Bob Clopine

Thomas and Sandra Cook

Jack and Donna Damson

Pauline des Granges

Cynthia Diller

Bill and Carolyn Doherty

Pamela Dunn

William and Thalia Evenson

Ron and Myra Flick

Dan and Sylvia Freeman

Terry and Jim Gase

George and Alison Gildred

Alan Goddard and E. Ann Matchinske

Mr. and Mrs. W. R. Goddard

Gayle Gould

Bill and Sharon Griswold

Monika and Jack Hardy

Aldyn and Karen Hoekstra

Bernice Hollerbach

Karen Hunt

Rob Hutsel

Ross and Sharon Irwin

Helen Long

Mr. and Mrs. Michael Lorch

Dorothy and Alan Lord

Charles and Ellen MacVean

Nee W. Mah

Robert Mainiero

Linda Masys

Elizabeth and Louis Meyer

Robert and Joany Mosher

Eleanor Neely

James and Melanie Nickel

Dan Patel

Les Pendarvis

Jim and Barbara Peugh

John Rebelo

Charlotte Saleebey

Byron Schilling

Marcia Schofield

Steve and Nancy Stangland

Raymond Starr

Harris and Ardetta Steiner

Edward Streicher

John and Marcia Suter

Ed and LaVera Tye

Matt Wallace

Robert and Ginger Wallace